Quick Short Reference Gu

To

C/C++ Programming Concepts

Includes

C/C++ Tips and Concepts

Point-to-Point C/C++ Guide

Useful for all C/C++ Developers/Programmers

(N.PAUL)

Table of Contents

1 C++ OOP (Object-oriented programming)

Object-oriented programming (OOP) refers to a type of computer programming (software design) in which programmers define not only the data type of a data structure, but also the types of operations (functions) that can be applied to the data structure.

C++ is an object oriented programming language. C++ is a case sensitive programming language. The goal of object oriented programming is as follows:

- Clearer
- More reliable
- Easy maintenance of program

Basic concepts of OOP are:

Objects

- Is an instance of class
- Program objects should be chosen such that they match closely with the real world objects.
- When a program is executed, the objects interact by sending messages to one another.

Class

- Class is a collection of objects of similar type.
- Class is used to combine the data and operations of a structure into a single entity.
- Once a class has been defined, any number of object can be created.

Data Encapsulation

- Encapsulation is the mechanism that binds together code and the data it manipulates and keep both safe from outside interference and misuse.
- It groups all pieces of an object into one neat package.

Data Abstraction

- Data abstraction is taking only the essential features without including all the background information

Polymorphism

- "One interface multiple methods". It is nothing but the ability to take more than one forms depending upon the arguments passed to a function.

Inheritance

- Inheritance is a process by which objects of one class acquire the properties of objects of another class.
- The derived class inherits all the properties of the base class and has the properties of its own.

Dynamic binding

- This is also called lazy initialization or runtime binding or late binding.
- At runtime only, it would be decided, which derived class method is called.

2 C++ Advantages

- C++ is a highly portable language and is often the language of choice for multi-device, multi-platform app development.
- C++ is an object-oriented programming language and includes classes, inheritance, polymorphism, data abstraction and encapsulation.
- C++ has a rich function library.
- C++ allows exception handling, and function overloading which are not possible in C.
- C++ is a powerful, efficient and fast language. It finds a wide range of applications – from GUI applications to 3D graphics for games to real-time mathematical simulations.

3 C++ Program

C++ program, can be defined as a collection of objects that communicate via invoking each other's methods

```
#include <iostream>

using namespace std;

// main() is where program execution begins.

int main() {

cout << "Hello World"; // prints Hello World

return 0;

}
```

Here, "iostream.h" is the library used in C++ for all program execution. This indulges utilities like data input streaming, data output streaming...

There are two important objects of iostream class which are meant for the purpose.

- cin   //similar to printf() in C
- cout   //similar to scanf() in C

For example:

Say if a person wants to enter some value of a variable into the program, this could be done by the statement:

cin>>a;

Similarly, if a person wants to print some value on the screen, this could be done by the statement:

cout<<a;

Return 0; terminates main ( ) function and causes it to return the value 0 to the calling process.

In C++, the semicolon is a statement terminator.

4   C++ Tokens

A token is the smallest element of a C++ program that is meaningful to the compiler. The C++ parser recognizes these kinds of tokens: identifiers, keywords, literals, operators, punctuators, and other separators. A stream of these tokens makes up a translation unit.

Keyword: Keywords are predefined, reserved words used in programming that have a special meaning. Keywords are part of the syntax and they cannot be used as an identifier. Example: if, while, int etc.

Identifier: An identifier is used for any variable, function, data definition, etc. In the programming language C++, an identifier is a combination of alphanumeric characters, the first being a letter of the alphabet or an underline, and the remaining being any letter of the alphabet, any numeric digit, or the underline.

Constant: constants are treated just like regular variables except that their values cannot be modified after their definition. Constants can be any numeric, string or char value. Example: 123, 23, "c++", 'j' or 'k' or 'l' etc.

String: String composed of words separated by whitespace.

Operator: An operator is a symbol that tells the compiler to perform specific mathematical or logical manipulations. C++ is rich in built-in operators and provides the following types of operators: Arithmetic operator, logical operator and relational operator.

5   C++ Coding Standards

Standardization is very important at the time of coding. Everybody should follow defined coding standards to increase the readability of their code. A complex code with proper coding standards makes the code easy to understand for the programmer. A proper standardized code also helps the entire project to go-smooth. Using proper comments, following naming convention, proper documentation of the code make the entire code simple, readable and self-explanatory. Programmers can go into and easily find out what is going on inside the code and new people can also get up to code easily.

Now the question is whether standardize code is directly related to project success? No. It is not directly linked to project success but surely it helps a lot to make the whole project a successful one.

6   C++ Comments

Use of comments is also very much helpful to understand coding. Comments are the part of source code but they are disregarded by the Compiler. The programmer can use them to include short explanations or observations within the source code itself to make his/her code more readable.

C++ allows two ways of inserting comments:

// Single line comments

/* Multiple line comment

   Or Block comments */

Use comments before starting a Class, a file, a method. This type of comments gives the description about what the particular class, method is doing? It also mentions the purpose of the Class and gives other description.

7   C++ Identifiers

A C++ identifier is a name used to identify a variable, function, class, module, or any other user-defined item. An identifier starts with a letter A to Z or a to z or an underscore (_) followed by zero or more letters, underscores, and digits (0 to 9). C++ does not allow punctuation characters such as @, $, and % within identifiers.

8   C++ Keywords

Keywords are predefined, reserved words used in programming that have a special meaning. Keywords are part of the syntax and they cannot be used as an identifier. Example: if, while, int etc.

9   C++ Whitespace

Whitespace is the term used in C++ to describe blanks, tabs, newline characters and comments. Whitespace separates one part of a statement from another and enables the compiler to identify where one element in a statement, such as int, ends and the next element begins.

10   C++ NULL Statement

Any line of code not ending with semicolon is called a null statement in C++ because compiler does not recognize it as some executable line of code.

Hence, it is very important to put semicolon at the end of each line of code in C++.

11   C++ Data Types

Classifications of C++ Data Types:

- Basic data type: Such as int, float, char, long, double, long double, etc. are basic inherent data types of C++
- User-defined data type: Structure & Classes and Enum
- Derived data types: Arrays, Functions, Pointers etc.

12 C++ Variables

A variable provides the named storage that our programs can manipulate.

Example: Int i, j, k;

The line int i, j, k; both declares and defines the variables i, j and k; which instructs the compiler to create variables named i, j and k of type int.

13 C++ Local Vs Global Variables

Variables that are declared inside a function or block are local variables. They can be used only by statements that are inside that function or block of code.

Global variables are defined outside of all the functions, usually on top of the program. The global variables will hold their value throughout the life-time of your program.

14 C++ literals

A literal is some data that's presented directly in the code, rather than indirectly through a variable or function call. Constants refer to fixed values that the program may not alter and they are called literals.

15 C++ Operators

An operator is a symbol that tells the compiler to perform specific mathematical or logical manipulations. C++ is rich in built-in operators and provides the following types of operators:

Arithmetic operator: Addition +, Subtraction -, Multiplication *, Division /, Modulus %, Assignment =, Increment ++, Decrement --

Logical operator: AND &&, OR ||, NOT!

Relational operator: less than <, greater than >, equal to ==, not equal to != ,greater than or equal to >= , less than or equal to<=

Bitwise operator: bitwise and & ,bitwise or |,bitwise negate ~, left shift <<, right shift >>

Other operators: scope resolution::, indirection operator ->, new and delete, line feed operator endl, set width setw(n), n= number of spaces to be set

16 C++ Modifiers

A modifier is used to alter the meaning of the base type so that it more precisely fits the needs of various situations. There are four kinds of modifiers: Signed, Unsigned, Short and Long.

The modifiers can be combined. For example, you can use signed or unsigned with long or short modifiers. The correct use of modifiers can reduce the memory usage. So if we know that our variable can never be negative then to save memory we should use unsigned modifiers. And we should use short modifier if we know the range of variable will be below 32,767.

17 C++ Storage Classes

Storage classes are used to manage the lifetime and scope of the variables. A variable can have only one storage class. There are 4 types of the storage classes:

Automatic: By default C++ uses automatic storage. The scope of an automatic variable is within the block where it is declared.

Static: The static storage can be used when you want to keep the value of local variable during the whole life of the program. The static variable once created will retain the value even if you exit the code block and enter it again.

Register: The register storage is used if you want faster access to the variable. The variable will get stored in the CPU register instead of RAM (memory). The other properties of the register storage are same as of automatic storage, except the location, where the variable is stored.

External: The external storage is used when you want to access a global variable/object which is defined in another file. We use extern to specify the compiler that the current object is defined somewhere else in other file and not in current file.

18 C++ Loops

A loop statement allows us to execute a statement or group of statements multiple times. C++ programming language provides the following types of loop to handle looping requirements:

WHILE Loop: Repeats a statement or group of statements while a given condition is true. It tests the condition before executing the loop body.

FOR Loop: Executes a sequence of statements multiple times and abbreviates the code that manages the loop variable.

Do..WHILE Loop: Like a while statement, except that it tests the condition at the end of the loop body.

Nested Loops: You can use one or more loop inside any another while, for or Do..While loop.

19 C++ Loop Control Statement

Loop control statements change execution from its normal sequence.

C++ supports the following control statements:

BREAK Statement: Terminates the loop or switch statement and transfers execution to the statement immediately following the loop or switch.

CONTINUE Statement: Causes the loop to skip the remainder of its body and immediately retest its condition prior to reiterating.

GOTO Statement: Transfers control to the labeled statement. Though it is not advised to use GOTO statement in your program.

20 C++ Conditional Statement

Conditional statement decide what statements to be executed and what statements should not be executed depending upon the specific condition

C++ provided following Conditional statements:

IF Statement: Based on a condition, IF statement allows us to control a program whether to execute specific statement or not. Condition can be true or false.

IF..ELSE Statement: This means that when IF condition is true then the statements within it will be executed, and when IF condition is false then statements within ELSE condition will be executed.

SWITCH Statement: A switch statement allows a variable to be tested for equality against a list of values.

21 C++ Functions:

In order to make the code more readable, complete task to be performed is broken down in to small modules or sub-routines. Each of the modules is called a function. A function is a group/block of statements that perform some operations. Every C++ program has at least one function, which is main ().

When a program calls a function, program control is transferred to the called function. To call a function, you simply need to pass the required parameters along with function name. Three methods can be used to call a function: Call by Value, Call by reference and Call by Pointer.

Advantages of Function:

Dividing the program into functions (i.e. logical blocks) will make the code clear and easy to understand.

Functions are reusable i.e. you can call a function to execute same lines of code multiple times without re-writing it.

Individual functions are easy to maintain i.e. In case of any modification in the code you can modify only the function without changing the structure of the program.

22 C++ Arrays:

An array as a collection of variables of the same type. Arrays are fixed in size. Elements of an array will be allocated contiguously in memory. Elements of an array are accessed by an index. In simple words, an array is a fixed collection of similar objects stored contiguously and accessed by an index.

23 C++ Inline Function

Adding a prefix "inline" before a function definition is a request to the compiler to make the function inline; i.e. When the function is actually called, the line is replaced by the function definition itself while making executable file.

This is because the overhead of putting the small functions in stack and popping while executing is comparatively more. So, compiler checks if optimization could be done and accordingly makes the function inline.

Remember: inline is not a command to the compiler, just a request.

The compiler may or may not execute the function as inline which is actually decided internally by the compiler as which would be the most optimized way of execution in terms of time and space.

Also, any function defined within a class (without adding the word "inline") is by default inline request to the compiler for that particular function.

Inline function will not work in below cases:

1. With Loop/switch/goto
2. For function not returning values, if return statement exist
3. Function containing static variables
4. With recursive functions

24 C++ Namespace

A namespace is a container for identifiers. A namespace is a declarative region that provides a scope to the identifiers (the names of types, functions, variables, etc.) inside it. Namespaces are used to organize code into logical groups and to prevent name collisions that can occur especially when your code base includes multiple libraries.

A namespace is designed to overcome this difficulty and is used as additional information to differentiate similar functions, classes, variables etc. with the same name available in different libraries. Using namespace, you can define the context in which names are defined. In essence, a namespace defines a scope.

25 C++ Classes & Objects

The classes are the most important feature of C++ that leads to Object Oriented programming. Class is a user defined data type, which holds its own data members and member functions, which can be accessed and used by creating instance of that class.

The variables inside class definition are called as data members and the functions are called member functions.

For example: Class of birds, all birds can fly and they all have wings and beaks. So here flying is a behavior and wings and beaks are part of their characteristics. And there are many different birds in this class with different names but they all possess this behavior and characteristics.

Similarly, class is just a blue print, which declares and defines characteristics and behavior, namely data members and member functions respectively. And all objects of this class will share these characteristics and behavior.

An object is a member or an "instance" of a class. An object has a state in which all of its properties have values that you either explicitly define or that are defined by default settings.

26 C++ Inheritance

Inheritance is the capability of one class to acquire properties and characteristics from another class. The class whose properties are inherited by other class is called the Parent or Base or Super class. And, the class which inherits properties of other class is called Child or Derived or Sub class.

Inheritance makes the code reusable. When we inherit an existing class, all its methods and fields become available in the new class, hence code is reused.

Inheritance Visibility Mode:

Public Inheritance: This is the most used inheritance mode. In this the protected member of super class becomes protected members of sub class and public becomes public.

Private Inheritance: In private mode, the protected and public members of super class become private members of derived class.

Protected Inheritance: In protected mode, the public and protected members of Super class becomes protected members of Sub class.

Base Class	Derived Class Public Mode	Derived Class Private Mode	Derived Class Protected Mode
Private	Not Inherited	Not Inherited	Not Inherited
Protected	Protected	Private	Protected
Public	Public	Private	Protected

In C++, There are five different types of Inheritance:

Single Inheritance: In this type of inheritance one derived class inherits from only one base class. It is the simplest form of Inheritance.

Multiple Inheritance: In this type of inheritance a single derived class may inherit from two or more than two base classes.

Hierarchical Inheritance: In this type of inheritance, multiple derived classes inherits from a single base class.

Multilevel Inheritance: In this type of inheritance the derived class inherits from a class, which in turn inherits from some other class. The Super class for one, is sub class for the other.

Hybrid (Virtual) Inheritance: Hybrid Inheritance is combination of Hierarchical and Multilevel Inheritance.

27 C++ Constructors

Constructors are special class functions which performs initialization of every object. The Compiler calls the Constructor whenever an object is created. The name of constructor will be same as the name of the class, and constructors never have return type. Constructors can be defined either inside the class definition or outside class definition using class name and scope resolution "::" operator.

In C++, There are three different types of Constructors:

Default Constructor: Default constructor is the constructor which doesn't take any argument. It has no parameter.

Parameterized Constructor: These are the constructors with parameter. Using this Constructor you can provide different values to data members of different objects, by passing the appropriate values as argument.

Copy Constructor: These are special type of Constructors which takes an object as argument, and is used to copy values of data members of one object into other object.

Characteristics of Constructor:

- They are to be declared under public section
- They are invoked automatically once objects are created.
- They do not have any return types, not even return type "void".
- Like other C++ function, they can have default arguments.
- Constructor cannot be virtual.
- We cannot refer to their addresses.
- An object with constructor/destructor can't be used as member of any function.
- They make implicit class to the operators new and delete when memory allocation I s required.

28 C++ Destructors

Destructor is a special class function which destroys the object as soon as the scope of object ends. The destructor is called automatically by the compiler when the object goes out of scope.

The syntax for destructor is same as that for the constructor, the class name is used for the name of destructor, with a tilde ~ sign as prefix to it. Destructors will never have any arguments.

Characteristics of Destructor:

- A destructor never any arguments.so we cannot overload destructors.
- They do not have return types, not even void
- A destructor will be invoked implicitly by the complier upon exit from the program to clean up storage that is no longer accessible.
- Destructor can be virtual but Constructor cannot be virtual.

29 C++ Function Overloading

If any class have multiple functions with same names but different parameters then they are said to be overloaded.

Function overloading is usually used to enhance the readability of the program. If you have to perform one single operation but with different number or types of arguments, then you can simply overload the function.

Function can be overloaded either by changing number of Arguments or by having different types of argument.

30 C++ Operator Overloading

Operator overloading—less commonly known as operator ad hoc polymorphism—is a specific case of polymorphism, where different operators have different implementations depending on their arguments. Operator overloading is generally defined by the language, the programmer, or both.

For example '+' operator can be overloaded to perform addition on various data types, like for Integer, String (concatenation) etc.

Rules for overloading operators

1. Only existing operators can be overloaded.

2. The overload operator must have at least on operand that is of user defined type.

New operators cannot be created.

3. We cannot change basic meaning of any operator i.e we cannot use + for subtraction

4. Overload operators follow the syntax rules of original operators. They can't be over ridden.

5. Sizeof,.(membership operator),. *(pointer to member operator), :: (scope resolution operator),?: (conditional operator) can't be overloaded.

6. = (assignment operator), ()(function call operator),[] (subscripting operator),-> (class member access operator) can't be overloaded using friend functions.

31 C++ Abstraction

Data abstraction provides only essential information to the outside world and hiding their background details. Abstraction is one of the main concepts of the Object Oriented Programming. A class represents an "entity" that can communicate with other classes or functions. But, class can hide information about its data and behavior. It can be done by using private data members and functions. Class should provide access to only necessary information which is useful outside the class and we should hide its internal representation.

A class communicates with the outer world by using public data member functions. These member functions are often called **interface** of a class. When you design a class, you should separate the **implementation** of a class with its interface. This will give you a possibility to easily change the behavior of the class without changing the interface code.

Data abstraction increases the effectiveness of programs. For example: If you have a car and car gets start by putting the key. There is no need to understand how fuel comes from the tank inside the engine of a car and how it catches fire using a spark plug and how wheels rotate after combustion of fuel inside engine. All these details are abstracted from you when you drive a car. Because of these abstractions you can effectively drive a car because only essential information are visible to you that make you drive easily.

32 C++ Encapsulation

Encapsulation is the idea of hiding the details of how things are implemented without exposing full interface to the user. This allows the user to use the item without worrying about how it is implemented.

In Object Oriented Programming, encapsulation represents binding data and functions into one container. This container hides the details of the data and the way functions process data.

33 C++ Polymorphism

The word polymorphism means having multiple forms of one thing. In Object Oriented Programming, polymorphism represents possibility to have multiple implementations of the same functions. The most interesting concepts of polymorphism are related to Inheritance. A pointer of base class can be used as pointer of derived class.

34 C++ Exception Handling

During the process of coding, the user may come across some errors which may be syntactically correct but may still give an undesired output. Such errors are which occur only when a specific condition is true are known as Exceptions.

There are mainly two types of Exceptions:

1) Synchronous: The simplest example of such an exception is 'Divide by Zero' error. When a number is divided by zero it results in an undefined error (Exception) which is not handled by the compiler and rather needs to be taken care of by the Developer.

2) Asynchronous: These types of exceptions cannot be controlled by the developer, such as Interrupts.

In C++ exceptions are handled using the try-catch block. The basic idea behind this block is that

First, the code to be executed is put in the TRY block.

Second, if an exception occurs then it is THROWN.

Finally, the exception thrown is caught by the CATCH block and handled appropriately.

NOTE: if no exception occurs in the TRY block then the CATCH block is never executed.

- When any exception object is generated and thrown, that exception is caught by corresponding catch statement, which processes the exception.
- We can write more than one catch statement associated with a try.
- Which catch statement to be invoked is to be determined by exception type.
- When an exception is caught, argument variable will receive its value.
- Any type of data could be possible caught, including classes that you create.

- If no exception is thrown (no error occurs within the try block), then none of the
- Catch statement gets executed.
- Throw generates the exception class object.
- If that exception has to be caught, then throw must be executed either from within a try, or from any called function within the try block (directly or indirectly).
- If your code is generating an exception for which there is no applicable catch statement, an abnormal program termination may occur.
- The terminate () function is called whenever the exception handling subsystem fails to find a matching catch statement for an exception.
- It is also called if your program attempts to re throw an exception when no exception was originally thrown.
- Throwing an unhandled exception causes the standard library function terminate () to be invoked.
- By default, terminate() calls abort() to stop your program
- A try block can be used inside a function.
- We can write more than one catch associated with a try. However, each catch must be defined to catch a different type of exception.

35 C++ Late Binding

Late binding is also known as Dynamic Binding or Runtime Binding.

Sometimes compiler can't know which function will be called till program is executed (runtime). This is known as late binding.

Binding is the process which is used by the compiler to convert identifiers (such as variable and function names) into machine language addresses.

It is a mechanism in which the method called by an object gets associated by name in runtime. Late binding happens when virtual keyword is used in member function declaration.

36 C++ References

Reference variable is simply another name for already existing object. References can be mistaken for pointers. It's not correct because references are less powerful than pointers. But references are safer than pointers.

Some important differences between C++ references and pointers:

References must be initialized once they are declared. So, a reference can't be NULL

Once a reference is declared and initialized there is no possibility to make reference variable to reference another object.

Pointers can point to no-where (NULL) but a reference always refers to some object.

We cannot take the address of the reference as we can do it with pointers.

You cannot do reference arithmetic like we can do with pointers.

Reference variables and Reference parameters:

A reference is essentially an implicit pointer.

A reference can be used: as a function parameter, as a function return value, or as a stand-alone reference.

By default, C++ uses call-by-value, but it provides two ways to achieve call-by-reference Parameter passing. First, you can explicitly pass a pointer to the argument. Second, you can use a reference parameter.

When you create an independent reference, all you are creating is another name for an object variable. All independent references must be initialized at the time of creation.

A base class reference can point to an object of a derived class.

Restrictions to References

You cannot reference another reference (we can't obtain address of reference)

It won't be possible to create arrays of references nor create a pointer to a reference nor reference a bit-field.

A reference variable once declared must be initialized unless it is member of a class or a function parameter or return value.

Null references are prohibited

37 C++important Points

1. C++ is a case sensitive programming language.

2. In C++, the semicolon is a statement terminator.

3. C++ supports single-line and multi-line comments. All characters available inside

    any comment are ignored by C++ compiler.

4. Any line of code not ending with semicolon is called a null statement in C++

5. The "endl" keyword is used to inserts a new-line character after every line.

6. The global variables will hold their value throughout the life-time of your program.

7. All four modifiers can be applied to the int type

8. char type allows only signed and unsigned modifiers

9. double type can be used with the long modifier

10. The modifiers can be combined. For example, you can use signed or unsigned with long or short modifiers.

11. Variable must be declared before they are used. Usually it is preferred to declare them at the starting of the program.

12. Constants refer to fixed values that the program may not alter and they are called **literals**.

13. The variables inside class definition are called as data members and the functions are called member functions.

14. Class's member functions can be defined inside the class definition or outside the class definition

15. Class in C++ are similar to structures in C, the only difference being, class defaults to private access control, whereas structure defaults to public.

16. All the features of OOPS, revolve around classes in C++. Inheritance, Encapsulation, Abstraction etc.

17. Objects of class holds separate copies of data members. We can create as many objects of a class as we need.

18. Objects are instances of class, which holds the data variables declared in class and the member functions work on these class objects.

19. Objects are initialized using special class functions called Constructors.

20. Whenever the object is out of its scope, another special class member function called Destructor is called, to release the memory reserved by the object.

21. A class definition starts with the keyword class followed by the class name; and the class body, enclosed by a pair of curly braces.

22. A class member can be defined as public, private or protected. By default members would be assumed as private.

23. The public data members of objects of a class can be accessed using the direct member access operator (.)

24. Private and protected members cannot be accessed directly using direct member access operator (.)

25. A class constructor is a special function in a class that is called when a new object of the class is created.

26. A destructor is also a special function which is called when created object is deleted.

27. The copy constructor is a constructor which creates an object by initializing it with an object of the same class, which has been created previously.

28. Every object has a special pointer this which points to the object itself.

29. A pointer to a class is done exactly the same way a pointer to a structure is. In fact a class is really just a structure with functions in it.

30. Both data members and function members of a class can be declared as static.

31. Member functions are the functions, which have their declaration inside the class definition and works on the data members of the class.

32. The definition of member functions can be inside or outside the definition of class.

33. A friend function is permitted full access to private and protected members of a class.

34. With an inline function, the compiler tries to expand the code in the body of the function in place of a call to the function.

35. Inheritance makes the code reusable. When we inherit an existing class, all its methods and fields become available in the new class, hence code is reused.

36. All members of a class except Private, are inherited

37. Purpose of Inheritance is: Code Reusability, Method Overriding, Use of Virtual keyword.

38. We can break an infinite loop using control statements like BREAK and GOTO.

39. Arrays are fixed in size.

40. Elements of an array will be allocated contiguously in memory

41. Elements of an array are accessed by an index.

42. Abstraction separates code into interface and implementation. So while designing your component, you must keep interface independent of the implementation so that if you change underlying implementation then interface would remain intact.

43. To make class members private by default unless we really need to expose them is a good example of encapsulation.

44. Late binding is also known as Dynamic Binding or Runtime Binding.

45. Inline function may not work if it contains any loop (s), switch, GOTO, static variables.

46. A static member function cannot be 'virtual'.

47. The key word "this" is a local variable present in any non-static function body.

48. "this" refers to current class object.

49. The keyword "this" does not need declaration and is rarely referred to explicitly in a function definition.

50. Function overriding stop inheritance.

51. A pure virtual function is a virtual function that has no definition within the base class.

52. Abstract Class is a class that contains at least one pure virtual function.

53. We cannot create objects of an abstract class.

54. We can create pointers and references to an abstract class.

55. If no exception occurs in the TRY block then the CATCH block is never executed.

56. A function or entire class can be declared as friend of another class.

57. Pointers are simple references to non-contiguous memory location. It stores address of some other variable and points to its values.

58. We can use typedef to define type of some long variable type.